HORSEBACK RIDING is for me

HORSEBACK RIDING is for me

text by
Art Thomas and
Emily Blackburn

photographs by
Art Thomas and
Tom Galvin

 Lerner Publications Company   Minneapolis

Art Thomas wishes to thank Linda Bumbulis and the members of her family and the staffs of Rocky River, Ohio, and Sunrise stables.
Emily Blackburn wishes to thank Carey Radtke and Bill Nunn.
Cover photograph by Carl Badger

*In memory of Joseph Bumbulis
and Maureen Smith*
> — *A.T.*

For Carol
> — *E.B.*

LIBRARY OF CONGRESS CATALOGING IN PUBLICATION DATA

Thomas, Art, 1952-
Horseback riding is for me.

(A Sports for me book)
SUMMARY: Follows a young rider as she learns the fundamentals of horsemanship including posting, dismounting, and grooming.

1. Horsemanship—Juvenile literature. [1. Horsemanship]
I. Blackburn, Emily, joint author. II. Title. III. Series:
Sports for me books.

SF309.2.T49   1981   798.2'3   80-13081
ISBN 0-8225-1092-8   (lib. bdg.)

Manufactured in the United States of America

International Standard Book Number: 0-8225-1092-8
Library of Congress Catalog Card Number: 80-13081

2   3   4   5   6   7   8   9   10   85   84   83   82

Hi! My name is Linda. And this is Okie.
I ride Okie almost every day. I'd like to tell
you about her and about horseback riding.

I've always loved horses. Many years ago,
I began collecting model horses. Then I
began reading all I could about horses.
Every Saturday I went to the stables near
our home and watched people ride. Their
horses looked so beautiful and graceful. I
looked forward to the day I could take
riding lessons.

One day while I was visiting the stables, I met Maureen. Maureen owned a horse named Okie, and she took very good care of her. She made sure she was fed properly and that her **stall** was cleaned regularly. A stall is a compartment inside a barn. One horse lives in each stall. Maureen also brushed Okie every day. She said this, too, was part of taking care of a horse.

Maureen told me that beginners should take riding lessons so they can learn the proper way to ride and care for a horse. She explained that there are two basic kinds of riding, **English** and **Western**, and that she rode English.

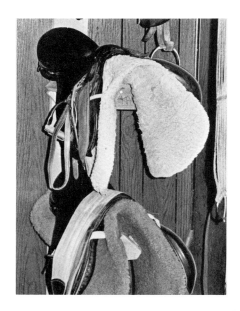 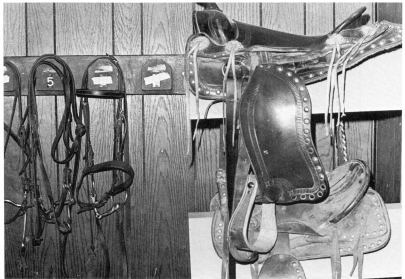

I already knew a little about Western riding, but I didn't know anything about English. So Maureen began by showing me her **tack**, which is all the equipment used for riding a horse.

English tack is different from Western tack. Here is an English **bridle**. The bridle goes on the horse's head. The **bit**, the metal mouthpiece on the bridle, fits into the horse's mouth, over its tongue.

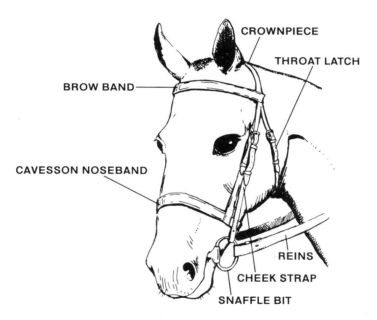

CROWNPIECE

THROAT LATCH

BROW BAND

CAVESSON NOSEBAND

REINS

CHEEK STRAP

SNAFFLE BIT

This is a **snaffle** bit. Because a snaffle is hinged in the middle, it is more comfortable for the horse than other types of bits. The bit is held in place by leather straps that go around the horse's head. Also attached to the bit are **reins**, which are held by the rider and help him or her control the horse.

The rider sits in the **saddle**. The saddle is held in place on the horse by a long strap called a **girth**. The underside of a saddle is designed to fit the horse, and the topside is designed to fit the rider. The rider's feet go in the **stirrups**, which are attached to the saddle by long leather straps.

I asked my parents if I could take riding lessons. They said it was okay if I would do extra work around the house to help pay for them. The work wasn't much fun, but I didn't mind because I knew riding lessons were expensive.

The next Saturday Maureen took me to the stables to sign up for lessons. She introduced me to Nancy, my teacher, who was very friendly. Then Maureen told me I could ride Okie if I would help her take care of her. I was really excited because Okie was my favorite horse.

Maureen told me that more experienced riders usually ride in special clothes. Most beginning riders, though, wear jeans and an old pair of shoes or boots. These shoes or boots should have heels on them to keep the rider's feet from slipping through the stirrups.

At our first lesson, we watched Nancy put the tack on our horses. She said that we would be able to do this ourselves after we had learned how. The girls and boys in my class who didn't own their own horses rode horses that belonged to the stables. I sure felt lucky to have Okie to ride!

First, we got acquainted with our horses by talking to them and patting them. I learned to put one hand on Okie's rump when I had to walk behind her so she would know I was back there.

Next, we led our horses inside a **ring**. The ring is an area that is enclosed by a fence. At our stables there is also a building called an **indoor arena** used for riding inside.

The first thing we learned in the ring was to walk on the left side of our horses when leading them and to keep a lot of space between each horse. After we led our horses around for a few minutes, we learned how to **mount**, or get on them. I soon found out that mounting was a lot harder than it looked!

Mounting is done in several steps, but it should look like one smooth movement. I began by standing on Okie's left side, the proper side to mount from. I gathered the reins in my left hand so they were fairly tight but not pulling on Okie's mouth. This way, I could control her if she started to walk away before I was in the saddle.

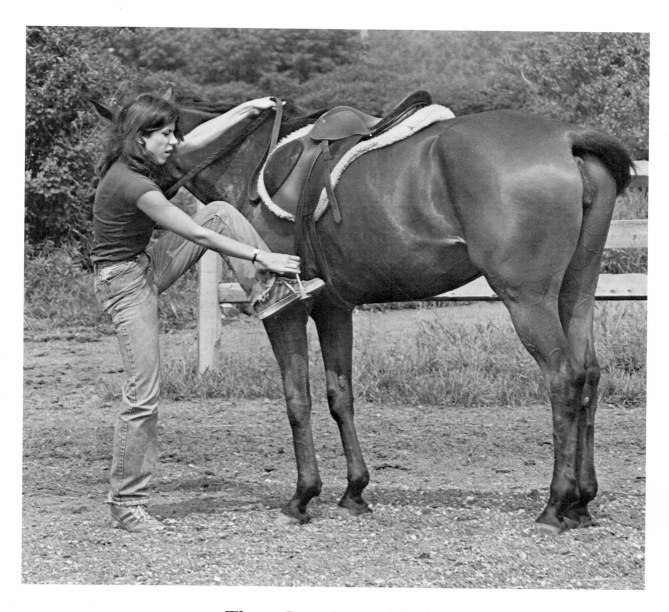

Then, I took my left hand with the reins in it and grabbed some of Okie's mane in front of the saddle. Next, I turned the stirrup clockwise with my right hand and lifted my left foot into it. The step between the ground and the stirrup sure was big!

Then came the hard part. With my left foot in the stirrup, I placed my right hand on the back of the saddle, or **cantel**. I made a few small hops on my right foot, lifted it off the ground, and pulled myself up.

Next, I lifted my right hand and placed it on the front of the saddle, or **pommel**, as I swung my right leg over Okie's back. (The right leg shouldn't touch the saddle or the horse.) Then I eased myself down until I was sitting in the saddle. Nancy said it is very important *never* to thump down into the saddle because this can hurt the horse's back.

After I was sitting in the saddle, I put my right foot in the stirrup. The balls of the rider's feet should rest in the stirrups with the toes pointed forward and the heels down. Next, I gathered the reins in both hands, and Nancy showed me how to hold them.

 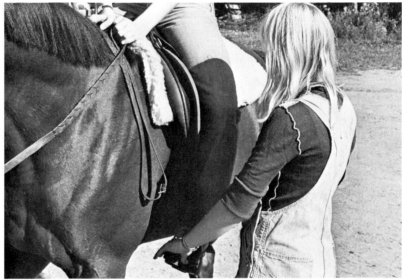

I held my hands in a loose fist with my thumbs on top. The reins came up between my little fingers and my ring fingers and out the top between my thumbs and index fingers. Then Nancy adjusted my stirrups to the proper length. She explained that when my legs were hanging straight down, the bottom of my stirrups should be just below my ankle bones.

As soon as Nancy finished adjusting our stirrups, she explained how to **dismount**, or get off. She said we should do just the opposite of what we had done to mount.

With my left hand holding the reins and resting on Okie's neck, I stood up, swung my right leg over Okie's back, and then placed my right hand on the cantel. With my weight on my arms, I took my left foot out of the stirrup and dropped gently to the ground.

We practiced mounting and dismounting a few more times until we felt more comfortable doing it. Nancy said it would take a lot of practice before we could make it look smooth and easy.

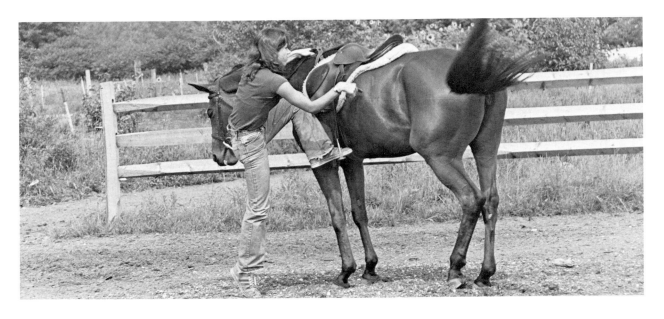

Finally, we were ready to **walk** forward. We did this by squeezing our legs against our horses' sides and relaxing the reins. When I did this, Okie walked forward. I was so excited to be moving! As we walked, Nancy explained the correct body position.

She said we should sit up straight with our chins up and heels down. Our legs should be directly underneath us for good balance, and our hips should be relaxed. Nancy said our hands should be relaxed but steady so that we would have steady **contact**, or touch, with our horses' mouths through the reins.

To turn right, I learned to move my right hand slightly to the right while keeping steady pressure on the left rein. At the same time, I brought my left leg back and then put pressure on Okie's right side with my right leg.

This way, Okie could bend around my right leg while my left leg kept her hindquarters from moving outward. To turn left, I applied the same **aids**, or signals, but in the opposite direction.

To bring Okie to a **halt**, or to stop her, Nancy told me to push my seat down and slightly forward, while increasing contact with Okie's mouth by steadying my fingers.

Because Okie felt resistance to her forward movement, she quietly halted. I was learning that if I gave the correct aids to Okie, she would know just what I wanted her to do.

When all of us felt comfortable walking our horses, Nancy said we were ready to **trot**. The trot is a two-beat **gait**, or forward movement, that is faster than the walk. To get our horses to trot, we simply squeezed harder with our legs and relaxed the pressure on the reins.

Since the trot is a springy gait, it is bouncy
for the rider. In order to make it easier for
both horse and rider, Nancy taught us how
to **post**, or move up and down in the saddle
in rhythm with the horse's movement. She
explained that when the horse's outside
foreleg (the front leg farthest from the center
of the ring) moves forward, the rider rises
up out of the saddle.

Most of the rider's weight should be on his or her knees and thighs. When the outside foreleg hits the ground, the rider sits back in the saddle. While trotting, the horse's head remains steady, so Nancy said our hands should also remain steady, keeping light contact with the horse's mouth.

I had a hard time learning how to post. I kept losing my balance. Nancy said it takes beginning riders many hours of practice before posting feels natural. We practiced posting the trot until Nancy told us it was time to quit for the day. Then we all walked our horses with our reins loose so they could relax.

After this, we dismounted, took off the saddles, and led our horses around the ring until they were completely cool and dry. Just as people need time to cool off after exercising, so do horses. A hot horse that is put in its stall and allowed to drink water or eat grain can become very sick.

Since Maureen had asked me to help her take care of Okie, she showed me how to **groom**, or brush, her. First, we took Okie's bridle off of her and put her **halter** on so she would be more comfortable. A halter is the headgear used for handling a horse when you're not riding it. Then I gave Okie a carrot and thanked her for doing such a good job for me in my lesson.

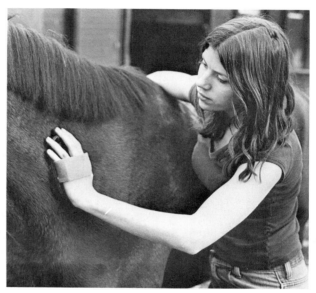

The first brush we used was a rubber brush called a **rubber curry.** We used this brush in a circular motion on Okie's neck and body to loosen dirt and dead hair. Maureen said a rubber curry is too hard to use on Okie's head and legs and we would use different brushes for that.

Next, we used a stiff **dandy brush** to remove all of this dirt and dead hair. We also used the dandy brush to clean Okie's legs.

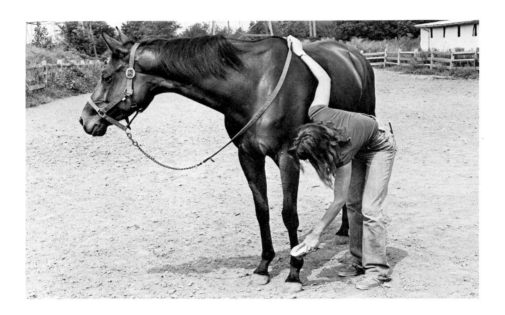

The last brush, a **body brush**, was a soft one that we used to make Okie's coat shine. We also used the body brush to clean Okie's head. Then I combed Okie's mane and tail with a metal comb. The last thing Maureen showed me was how to clean out Okie's hooves with a **hoof pick**.

Maureen said that grooming Okie would not only make her look really nice, but it would give Okie and me a chance to spend more time together. And the more time Okie and I could spend together, the better we would get to know each other. The friendship and trust that we developed would make riding much more enjoyable for both of us.

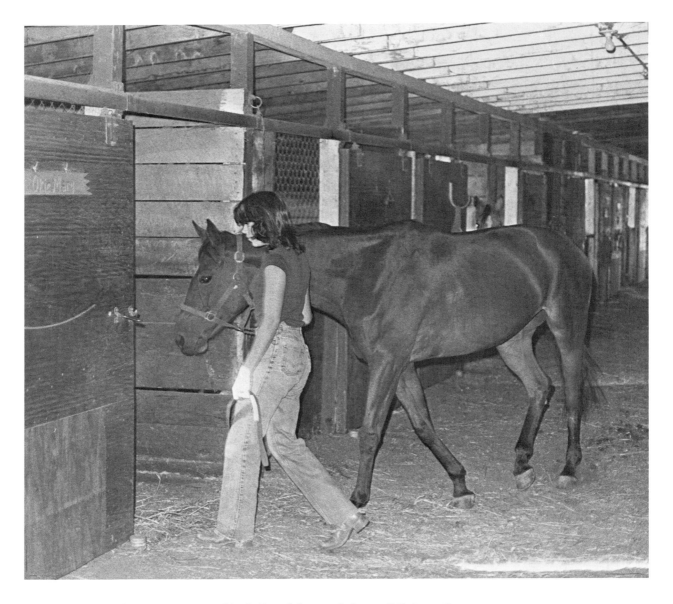

By the time we finished brushing Okie, she was ready to go back into her stall. Maureen gave her fresh water and then told me how much food Okie was given each day. People who work at the stables give hay and grain to the horses every day. They also turn the horses out into a **pasture**, or grassy field, so that they can eat grass.

Later that week, Maureen showed me how to put Okie's bridle and saddle on her. To put on the bridle, the bit is held in the rider's left hand, and the straps near the **crownpiece**, or top of the bridle, are held in the right hand.

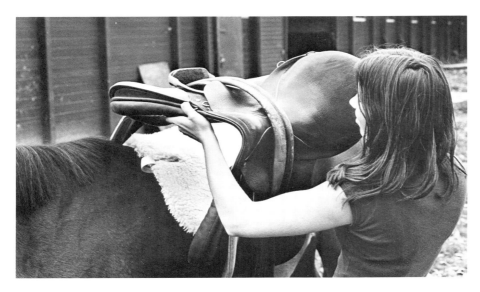

The bit is then slipped into the horse's mouth, and the crownpiece is put over its ears. Then Maureen showed me how to slide the saddle into place and fasten the girth.

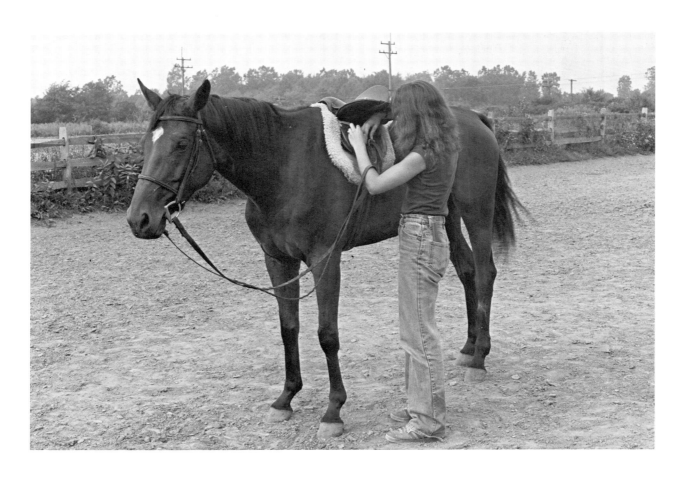

After a few weeks, Nancy told us we were ready to learn how to **canter.** The canter is a three-beat gait that is faster and smoother than the trot. A horse naturally leads with one or the other of its forelegs when cantering. The rider can determine which leg the horse will lead with by the aids he or she uses. When cantering in a ring, the horse's inside leg should lead.

Nancy explained the aids for cantering as well as the position of the rider. We had a chance to practice cantering one at a time, and I was the first one to try it.

As soon as Okie was trotting along the rail to the left, I brought my right leg back and then squeezed hard on Okie's left side with my left leg. I also sat deep in the saddle and pushed my seat forward. At the same time, I put a little bit of pressure on the left rein.

When I applied these aids, Okie cantered on the left lead. I felt like I was in a rocking chair! I sat with my back straight and my seat deep in the saddle. I followed the movement of the canter with my hips, and I kept my legs tight against Okie's sides so she wouldn't slow down.

The horse's head bobs slightly when it is cantering. In order to keep contact with Okie's mouth, I had to keep my hands steady. To canter to the right, I applied the same aids but in the opposite direction. Cantering was a lot of fun. It felt so free and easy!

We didn't always ride in the ring during our lessons. Sometimes we went for **trail rides** in the woods around the stables. Trail riding is much different than riding in the ring because you are not in an enclosed area. I really enjoyed riding in the woods, and I could tell that Okie did too—it was a nice change from ring riding.

I find that with every lesson I want to learn more and more about horses and riding. Sometimes I go to horse shows to see riders compete against one another.

Besides performing at the walk, the trot, and the canter, some riders also jump their horses over fences. I can hardly wait until I can enter my first horse show!

I'm still taking riding lessons from Nancy.
Now I'm in the intermediate class and am
learning how to jump.

My parents gave me a riding outfit for my birthday. My riding clothes and boots are much more comfortable to ride in than what I was wearing before. I even have a **hard hat** to protect my head in case I fall off Okie.

I hope someday I can have a horse of my own. I know that a horse is expensive to keep and will take up a lot of my time, too. But owning my own horse will help me become a better rider and will mean I'll have a special friend to take care of. Until then, though, I can ride Okie, who has sure helped me to know that horseback riding is for me!

HORSEBACK RIDING Words

AIDS: The signals the rider gives to the horse so that it knows what to do

BIT: The metal part of the bridle that is inserted into the horse's mouth

BRIDLE: The horse's headgear that is used for riding

CANTER: One of three natural gaits (forward movements) of the horse. The canter is a three-beat gait.

GAIT: A sequence of foot movements by which a horse moves forward

GIRTH: The long strap that keeps the saddle in place on the horse's back

GROOM: To clean or brush a horse

HALTER: The headgear used for handling a horse when you're not riding it

HARD HAT: A helmet worn to protect the rider's head in case he or she falls off the horse. A hard hat should *always* be worn when jumping.

POST: An up-and-down movement performed by the rider in rhythm to a horse's trot. Posting is done only when the horse is trotting.

REINS: Long straps attached to the bit and held in the rider's hands. The reins help the rider control the horse.

SADDLE: The piece of equipment used for riding that is the seat for the rider

STALL: A compartment inside a barn. One horse lives inside each stall.

STIRRUPS: The footrests attached to a saddle

TACK: The equipment used for riding a horse such as a bridle and saddle

TROT: One of three natural gaits (forward movements) of the horse. The trot is a two-beat gait.

WALK: One of three natural gaits (forward movements) of the horse. The walk is a four-beat gait.

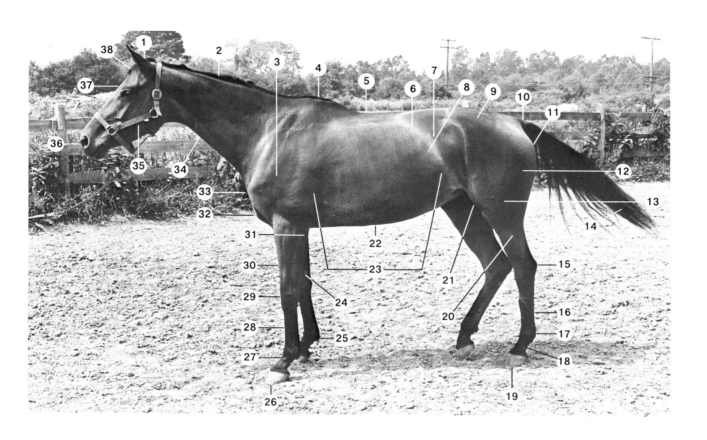

The Body of a Horse

1. POLL	11. POINT OF RUMP	21. STIFLE	31. ELBOW
2. MANE	12. BUTTOCK	22. BELLY	32. CHEST
3. SHOULDER	13. THIGH	23. BARREL	33. POINT OF SHOULDER
4. WITHERS	14. TAIL	24. CHESTNUT	34. NECK
5. BACK	15. HOCK	25. FETLOCK	35. CHEEK
6. LOIN	16. CANNON	26. HOOF	36. MUZZLE
7. POINT OF HIP	17. FETLOCK	27. PASTERN	37. FOREHEAD
8. FLANK	18. PASTERN	28. CANNON	38. FORELOCK
9. CROUP	19. HOOF	29. KNEE	
10. DOCK	20. GASKIN	30. FOREARM	

47

ABOUT THE AUTHORS

ART THOMAS is active in sports as an instructor, a participant, and a fan. As a drama and composition teacher in Cleveland, Ohio, Mr. Thomas is also involved with professional and community theater, both as an actor and a director. In addition, he writes travel and feature articles for newspapers and magazines and has authored several books. Mr. Thomas is also the co-photographer of this book.

EMILY BLACKBURN, an avid sportswoman, started riding at the age of 10. She has been working with horses ever since and rides both for pleasure and competition. Ms. Blackburn is currently employed as an editor for a book publishing company in Minneapolis, Minnesota.